Shiver Me Parsnips:

A Guide to Successful and Sustainable Vegetable Gardening in Zone 3

By Suzanne K. Peterson

2014 Edition

Copyright © 2014 Suzanne K. Peterson
All Rights Reserved

ISBN-13 978-1497465770
ISBN-10 149746577X

All Feedback Welcomed on   suzannepeterson83@yahoo.com

ACKNOWLEDGEMENTS

I would like to thank all of the members of my family for their help in getting this book published:

    To my parents David and Betty for their time in editing and reviewing this book

    To my brothers Richard and Randall for their patient review and inspiration

    To my niece Kelsey and my nephew Nick for their perspective and comments

    To my children David and Rebecca for correcting my grammar and helping me actually get the manuscript published.

DEDICATION

This book is dedicated to my Grandma, Elsie Stroschein, whose love for all things living inspired everyone she knew.

Preface

For many, the idea of sustainably growing vegetables in the Upper Midwest, especially in Zone 3, is intimidating. Some gardeners have had limited success, while others have failed miserably. And it always seems that what the seed packets say doesn't apply to Zone 3 gardens.

This book holds a solution for successfully and sustainably growing vegetables in the challenging Zone 3 climate. There are beautiful and bountiful home and market gardens even in this part of the U.S., and indeed in many other parts of the world with a similar climate. Most of that is due to adequate planning and realistic expectations.

Shiver Me Parsnips is a step by step guide for planning and growing a successful (and sustainable) vegetable garden in the short growing season available. It will help the novice gardener to focus on growing vegetables that will flourish and that they actually want to eat. It will reveal how long vegetables really take to grow in this climate, allowing for realistic expectations. It will explain simple and inexpensive means of season extension. And, by following the instructions in each chapter, it offers an easy to understand planning process to help ensure a thriving and rewarding garden experience.

How to Use This Book

Each chapter of this book can be read independently and used on its own merit. Following the instructions from beginning to end will allow any gardener to develop and put together a viable gardening plan based on the vegetables they want to grow. Any technical terms are marked by an asterisk and defined in the Glossary at the end of the book.

Chapters 10 and 11 contain additional information for those who want to go beyond a simple outdoor garden and try season extension or growing their own fresh produce in winter.

Chapter 12 is a compendium of handy tips and tricks used by successful gardeners in Zone 3. Using one or two of these tips alone could save more than the price of this book.

Table of Contents

Chapter 1	Background and Intended Audience	9
Chapter 2	Begin at the Beginning: Purpose and Goals for the Garden	14
Chapter 3	The Real Dirt on Soil Types	16
Chapter 4	Cornucopia: A Listing of Plants with Growing Guidance	20
Chapter 5	Getting Warmer: the Importance of Compost *	24
Chapter 6	As the Dirt Turns: Crop Rotation*and Companion Plants	25
Chapter 7	Caring for the Garden: Weeds, Water, and Weather	28
Chapter 8	Baby, Baby: Starting Seeds Indoors	30
Chapter 9	Putting it All Together	34
Chapter 10	It's Not Too Late Yet: Season Extension	36
Chapter 11	Growing in the Winter: Sprouts and Forcing	41
Chapter 12	Tips, Tricks, and Techniques	43

Appendix A USDA Hardiness Zone Map for Zones 3 and 4   47
Appendix B Theme Gardens   48
Appendix C Vegetable Quantity Calculation Guide   49
Appendix D Resources for Seeds and Planting Supplies   51
Appendix E Bibliography and Further Reading   52
Appendix F Glossary   54

Chapter 1   Background and Intended Audience

This book is intended to help home or small market growers successfully and sustainably raise vegetables in Zone 3. There are simple guidelines for someone just getting into gardening, and more detailed tips and tricks for more advanced gardeners. Many of the tables in this book are based on information I wish I had known when I was just starting to garden more seriously. Growers in zones 2 or 4 will also find the tables and tips useful. Using the information in this book should help every grower develop their individual garden growing plan, and have a productive, sustainable, and successful vegetable garden. In addition, gardeners in other parts of the world with a similar climate can apply the same principles to have a thriving garden.

Zone Definition

The USDA (United States Department of Agriculture) has divided the various areas of the U.S. into hardiness "Zones" based on coldest temperatures experienced during the year. Most of the Upper Midwest is in Zone 3 (minimum temperature -30F to -40F) or Zone 4 (minimum temperature of -20F to -30F). See the USDA Hardiness Zone Map in Appendix A. States with significant Zone 3 or 4 regions include: Montana, Wyoming, North Dakota, South Dakota, Minnesota, and Wisconsin. Parts of upstate New York, Vermont, New Hampshire, and Maine on the eastern seaboard also are considered Zone 3. Gardeners outside of the US who work in a similar climate include those living in parts of Russia, China, and Canada. A detailed worldwide hardiness zone map is available at: http://tcpermaculture.blogspot.com.

Even within the zones, however, growing conditions can vary (not to mention ongoing climate change). For example, someone who lives near the shore of a lake or river will have the mitigating effect of the water. Most yards or gardens have a variety of microclimates*. By paying attention to them in your own garden you can be more successful at growing plants which are marginal in Zone 3.

Sustainable Gardening

In order to garden sustainably, it is important to focus on leaving the ground in better condition than you find it each year. This means that you need to add compost* or other organic* matter, correct the pH* if necessary, and add any other minor minerals which are low or nonexistent in the soil. Having your soil tested is a good way to determine the current condition of your soil. You can use the results to plan what components need to be added over time. In the US, your local cooperative extension office often does soil sample testing for a reasonable fee. They also can provide information on what a nutrient deficiency looks like in the plants you grow, and can offer solutions when a deficit in some nutrient is found. As of March 2014 a basic soil test done by the University of Minnesota costs $15 with additional specialized tests ranging from $7-$18 for each additional item.

Pesticides and herbicides are generally not needed as long as the plants are healthy, and they are definitely not something anyone wishes to eat. Natural remedies are available in case of an insect infestation, and should be used if necessary. Rodale Press has many useful guides available, or simply search online for natural pest control. Several Pest Control Tips are also in the Tips, Tricks, and Techniques Chapter of this book.

There is an ongoing debate about whether or not to till the soil, and both sides of the issue have valid arguments. I cultivate my soil because it stays too cold for too long in my garden for me to go with a no-till type of method. I also start most of my seeds in the house and transplant later for the same reason. To be fair, I must point out that disturbing the soil does make the plants start out more slowly than in an untilled bed. The bed takes longer to warm up in the spring, however, which sometimes means the difference between getting a crop into the ground in time and getting it in too late or not at all. Experiment in your own garden and see what works best for you.

Basic Equipment

Now, let's talk about basic equipment. Every gardener needs tools, and the most important to have right away are a spade and a hoe. A spade (flat sided shovel) is needed for any kind of planting or other soil preparation which requires the soil to be turned over. Choose a spade with a sturdy handle which is long enough for you to use comfortably. Cleaned after use and protected from the elements, a good spade should last a long time. (I inherited a spade from my grandmother which I still use.)

There are many kinds of hoes, and the one you choose depends on how you like to use it to control weeds. Some people like to chop the weeds with an up and down motion, so they want a chopping style hoe. Chop hoes work well in heavy soil. Others prefer to cut weeds down with a back and forth motion, and so get a stirrup or diamond headed hoe. Stirrup hoes work better in lighter soil. It is important to choose the hoe that works best for you, and make sure it has a sturdy and comfortable handle. You will be using it a lot.

Figure 1 Chop Hoe

Figure 2 Garden Rake (top) and Diamond Headed Hoe

Figure 3 Top to Bottom Pitchfork, Spade, Shovel

After the spade and the hoe, the next most vital tools are a shovel, pitchfork, pruners, and a garden rake. A standard shovel does move dirt faster than a spade, so it can be a real time saver. A pitchfork is handy for moving mulch*, dry compost*, hay or straw. It can also be used to aerate* compacted soil. Pruners are valuable in harvesting crops so as not to damage them, cutting down plant stalks in the fall, and for controlling the growth of vigorous plants like tomatoes. A rake is useful for spreading compost* on existing beds or for smoothing out the soil surface in preparation for planting more seeds.

The last piece of basic equipment needed is a wheelbarrow or garden cart. It seems inevitable that something always needs to be hauled somewhere (dirt, compost*, mulch*, leaves, etc), and it is certainly easier on the back if it can be pulled or pushed rather than carried. If you don't have one already, choose which works better for you – a cart (if you like to pull the load) or a wheelbarrow (if you like to push the load). A cart tends to be easier on the back, while a wheelbarrow can go into narrower spaces. Regardless, get something which is sturdier than you think you will require. You want to be able to load it heavily sometimes without it breaking down on you.

Figure 4 Large Garden Cart

Additionally, a soil thermometer is indispensible when determining the best time to plant outside. It takes a lot of the guesswork out of how a plant will react when transplanted. Soil thermometers are available at most hardware stores or garden centers.

For those who are physically impaired or who have the means, a small tractor and utility trailer are extremely useful. These days, many implements are available for even small tractors which allow much of the manual labor to be minimized. You will need to plan your rows and plant spacing accordingly if you are going to cultivate or dig using machinery.

Chapter 2   Begin at the Beginning: Purpose and Goals for the Garden

The adage: "failure to plan is planning to fail" is very applicable to the Zone 3 garden. The warm days are so limited that you need to take advantage of each one of them.
 The first question to answer is: "What do I want to grow that I will actually want to eat?" Many great vegetables grow well in Zone 3, but if you don't like them – why bother? What you grow also has to be for the right reasons – that you actually like it. Growing all kinds of things so that you will eat healthier usually doesn't work very well. Neither will it be helpful to grow lots and lots of a vegetable which you only like a little bit, or which cannot successfully be preserved. Appendix B has examples of theme gardens (e.g. salsa garden, potato salad garden, etc.)

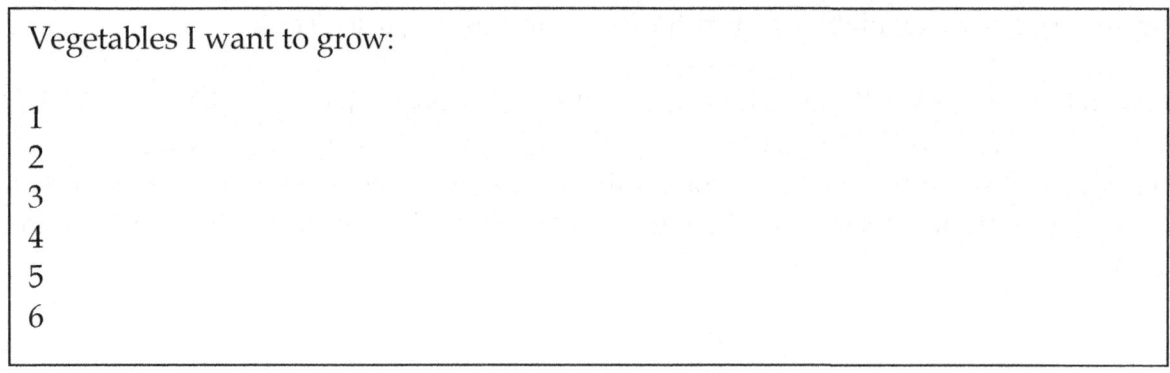

At least initially, limit yourself to focusing on a few of your favorite vegetables. As your expertise grows (and for the more experienced gardener) you can expand what you do. It is very important, especially initially, to grow something successfully. For the first five years at my farm my garden got smaller each year until it reached a size I could manage reasonably well. Also expect that there are some plants that simply will not do well in your soil. Don't despair, just try something else or find another gardener who is successfully growing what you want and trade with them. What a great opportunity for garden networking!

Once you know what you want to grow, then the next question to answer in the planning stage is: do I want some of these yummy veggies all summer, or do I want a whole bunch at once so I can preserve it for the winter? The tables in Appendix C will give you an idea of how much you need to grow of a particular vegetable to get a certain yield. It will also help you determine if it makes sense to preserve your bounty. Fill in the table below to document your plan.

Vegetable	Growing days	Desired Yield	Row feet* needed

You should plan to make the maximum use of your garden space by growing more than one crop in a given area if possible. Succession planting* can also ensure you can harvest your favorite vegetables for a longer period of time.

Now that you know how much space you need to grow your garden goodies, it's time to talk about their homeland – your soil.

Chapter 3   The Real Dirt on Soil Types

Although the weather may be the same above the soil, plants respond very differently to varying soil types. Basically, soils are either clay-based or sand-based, depending on what is their major constituent. And soil type can vary within a field or even within a garden space. It is important to know what type of soil you have so you can work with it, rather than fight it.

Here is one simple way to determine your soil type. After a rain of at least one inch, how long does it take for the water to completely soak into the ground? If it is less than a day, your soil is sandy. If it is more than three days, your soil is clay-based.

Although you can try to grow almost anything in either type of soil, some vegetables will do much better than others in their favorite soil type. It is important to keep this in mind, since trying to make something grow is a lot more work than simply helping it along in an environment it likes.

Here is a table listing the vegetable, their preferred soil type, and what do to help create it if you don't have it.

Vegetable	Preferred Soil Type	Aspect Veggie likes	Ways to help veggie	Notes
Green Bean	Sandy	Warm soil	Black plastic	
Wax Bean	Sandy	Warm soil	Black plastic	
Lima Bean	Sandy	Very Warm soil	Black plastic	
Beet	Clay	Cool Soil	Mulch*	Bolts* in hot weather
Broccoli	Clay	Cool Soil	Mulch*	Needs cool weather to form heads
Brussels Sprouts	Clay	Cool Soil	Mulch*	Needs cool weather to form sprouts
Cabbage	Clay	Cool Soil	Mulch*	Heads split in heat
Cardoon	Sandy	Drained, Warm	Black plastic	Blanch* stalks
Carrot	Clay for short, sandy for long	Cool soil	Mulch*	Slow growing initially
Cauliflower	Clay	Cool soil	Mulch*	Needs two cool months
Celeriac	Clay	Cool moist soil	Mulch*	Heavy feeder*
Celery	Clay	Cool moist soil	Mulch*	Heavy feeder*, long season
Swiss Chard	Clay	Cool Soil	Mulch*	Bolts* in hot weather
Chinese Cabbage	Clay	Cool Soil	Mulch*, shade	Bolts* in hot weather, long days
Collards	Sandy	Well drained soil	Drainage	Sweeter after frost
Corn	Sandy	Warm	Mulch*	Water sufficiently For optimum growth
Cucumber	Sandy	Warm	Mulch*, cold protection	Heavy feeder*
Eggplant	Sandy	Warm	Mulch*, cold protection	Needs full sun
Garlic	Sandy	Good Drainage		Keep slightly dry
Kale	Clay	Cool Soil	Mulch*	Take outside leaves for longer harvest
Kohlrabi	Clay	Cool Soil	Mulch*	Plant early so bulb develops when cool
Leek	Clay	Cool Soil	Mulch*, hill to blanch	Keep evenly moist, but not too wet
Lettuce	Clay	Cool Soil	Mulch*	Bolts* in hot weather

Vegetable	Preferred Soil Type	Aspect Veggie likes	Ways to help veggie	Notes
Muskmelon	Sandy	Warm Soil	Black Plastic	Stop watering when fruit ripens
Mustard	Clay	Cool Soil	Mulch*	Bolts* on long hot days
Okra	Sandy	Warm Soil	Black Plastic	Harvest often
Onion	Clay	Cool Soil	Mulch*	Long Day Varieties need long days for bulbs
Parsnip	Clay	Cool Soil	Mulch*	Long Cool Season
Pea	Clay	Cool Soil	Mulch*	Needs cool days to do well
Hot Pepper	Sandy	Warm Soil	Black Plastic, protection	Needs heat to grow well
Sweet Pepper	Sandy	Warm Soil	Black Plastic	Prefer some heat, but not too much
Potato	Clay	Cool fertile soil	Mulch*	Ideal pH* 5.5-6 (acid)
Pumpkin	Sandy	Warm Soil	Black Plastic compost* pile	Well drained soil high in organic* matter best
Radish	Clay	Cool Soil	Mulch*	Bolts* in long days
Rutabaga	Clay	Cool Soil	Mulch*	Need well worked soil
Spinach	Clay	Cool Soil	Mulch*	Keep uniformly moist
Summer Squash	Sandy	Warm Soil	Black Plastic	Needs warm soil to grow
Winter Squash	Sandy	Warm Soil	Black Plastic compost pile	Heavy feeder*
Tomatillo	Sandy	Warm Soil	Black Plastic Added heat	Needs long warm summer to produce fruit
Tomato	Sandy	Warm Soil	Black Plastic	Heavy Feeder*, needs sun
Turnip	Clay	Cool Soil	Mulch*	Too much nitrogen makes leaves not roots
Watercress	Clay	Moist Soil	Mulch*	Water Heavily
Watermelon	Sandy	Warm Soil	Black Plastic Added heat	Water well
Zucchini	Sandy	Warm Soil	Black Plastic	Needs warm soil to grow

Another important aspect of soil composition for your plants is organic* matter. Organic* matter is what actually feeds them, giving them many of the nutrients needed to grow. It is pretty hard to have too much organic* matter in the soil, but it must be of the kind that has decomposed* (rotted) enough to be available for the plants to use. Trying to plant potatoes in last fall's leaf pile won't work very well unless the leaves have actually decomposed* significantly. In order to continue sustainably growing vegetables in your garden, it is important to add decomposed* organic* matter (compost*) every time something new is planted. Making compost* is the subject of the Chapter 5.

Sometimes it may be necessary to use a commercially prepared supplement to feed your soil, especially if sufficient compost* is not available. If you buy a commercial fertilizer at the store it will usually have three numbers (e.g. 5-20-10). This means that it contains 5%N (Nitrogen), 20% P (Phosphorus), and 10% K (Potassium). Even commercially available organic* fertilizer will have these numbers listed. Based on your soil test, you should be able to choose a fertilizer which will supply whatever is lacking in your soil.

Chapter 4 Cornucopia: A Listing of Plants with Growing Guidance

The next item to consider is what kinds of plants to grow. The following table gives you an idea of what each vegetable likes, how long it actually takes to grow (based on experience growing in Zone 3), and any other special notes of interest. This is a brief and general summary of vegetables. Every year more interesting and exciting varieties become available.

Vegetable	Preferred Soil Characteristics	Ideal Transplant Age	Seed Catalog Days to Maturity	Usual Days to Maturity	Growing Conditions
Bush Bean	Warm soil to germinate	Doesn't Transplant well	55	70	Matures quickly and all at once, ideal for preservation
Pole Bean	Warm soil to germinate	Doesn't Transplant well	55	70	Needs support Longer harvest period ideal for eating fresh
Lima Bean	Warm, well worked to germinate	Doesn't Transplant well	65	80	Needs warmer soil than green beans
Beet	Loose, high in organic* matter	21 Days	50	60	Likes cool temperatures bolts* in heat, seedlings go to seed if too cold
Broccoli	Cool, fertile, pH* 6.5-7.5	35 Days	55	70	Needs cool temperatures to set heads*
Brussels Sprouts	Cool, fertile	35 Days	80	90	Needs long season to grow best to harvest after light frost
Cabbage	Cool, fertile, pH* 6.5-7.5	35 Days	55	70	Heads crack with heat or drought
Cardoon	Warm, well-drained	21 Days	80	90	Blanch* to tenderize stalks

Vegetable	Preferred Soil Characteristics	Ideal Transplant Age	Seed Catalog Days to Maturity	Usual Days to Maturity	Growing Conditions
Carrot	Cool, well worked	Doesn't Transplant well	50	70	Grows slowly when young, can be stored in ground under straw
Cauliflower	Cool, fertile	35 Days	55	80	Very intolerant of temperature extremes
Celeriac	Cool	35 Days	120	120	Likes cool nights, constant moisture
Celery	Cool	35 Days	100	110	Likes cool nights, needs blanching*
Swiss Chard	Cool, fertile, not acid	21 Days	55	55	Pick outer leaves for harvest all season
Chinese Cabbage (Bok Choy)	Cool	21 Days	30	45	Bolts* if shocked* or on hot days
Collards	Fertile, well drained	21 Days	75	75	Tolerates cold, heat
Corn	Warm, Fertile	Doesn't Transplant well	63	80	Needs heat to grow well
Cucumber	Warm, rich, well worked	14 Days	55	60	Needs warm soil to grow well, even moisture
Eggplant	Warm, rich,	56 Days	50	70	Needs a lot of heat to grow well
Garlic	Cool soil when small, well drained	Doesn't Transplant well	70	90	Keep somewhat dry, tolerates heat when larger
Kale	Cool, fertile, well drained	14 Days	55	60	Frost improves flavor, take outside leaves
Kohlrabi	Cool, fertile, well drained	14 Days	70	80	Prefers cool weather, even moisture
Leek	Cool, worked, well drained	56 Days	55	70	Blanch* for larger leeks, prefers cool temperature
Lettuce	Cool, good drainage	21 Days	35	40	Bolts* in heat or if crowded

Vegetable	Preferred Soil Characteristics	Ideal Transplant Age	Seed Catalog Days to Maturity	Usual Days to Maturity	Growing Conditions
Muskmelon	Warm, fertile	14 Days	85	90	Needs full sun and heat
Mustard	Cool, but sensitive to cold soil	21 Days	21	21	Bolts* in long days, some shade ok
Okra	Warm, Well drained	35 Days	45	50	Needs full sun, pick frequently
Onion	Fertile, Well worked	63 Days	35	35	Long Day varieties grow best
Parsnip	Cool, well worked	Doesn't Transplant well	90	110	Need long cool season to do well, slow to germinate
Pea	Cool, well drained	Doesn't Transplant well	55	60	Needs cool weather to grow well
Hot Pepper	Warm, well drained	56 Days	55	70	Needs warm soil and hot temperatures
Sweet Pepper	Warm, well drained	56 Days	55	70	Needs warm soil, warm temperatures
Potato	Cool, moist, pH* 5.0-5.5 ideal	Doesn't Transplant well	80	90	Needs long cool season to grow a lot of tubers*
Pumpkin	Warm, well drained	14 Days	95	95	Needs warm soil, but not too fertile
Radish	Cool, well worked, well drained	Doesn't Transplant well	35	40	Bolts* with long days, so cover midsummer
Rutabaga	Cool, moist	Doesn't Transplant well	90	100	Water evenly so roots don't get tough
Spinach	Cool, moist	21 Days	35	40	Bolts* in hot weather, partial shade ok
Summer Squash	Warm, well worked, heavy feeder*	14 Days	35	40	Use extra care when transplanting, lots of water when hot

Vegetable	Preferred Soil Characteristics	Ideal Transplant Age	Seed Catalog Days to Maturity	Usual Days to Maturity	Growing Conditions
Winter Squash	Warm, well worked, heavy feeder*	14 Days	95	95	Use extra care when transplanting, lots of water when hot
Tomatillo	Warm, full sun	35 Days	90	90	Needs long warm season to set fruit
Tomato	Warm, heavy feeder*	56 Days	55	70	Indeterminate* varieties must stake
Turnip	Cool, well drained	Doesn't Transplant well	45	45	Too much nitrogen grows leaves but not roots
Watercress	Cool, wet	14 Days	35	35	Keep very wet, pick leaves as needed
Watermelon	Warm, well drained	14 Days	85	90	Needs full sun, lots of heat
Zucchini	Warm, well worked soil	14 Days	35	40	Use extra care when transplanting

Plants that can tolerate some shade include: beets, kohlrabi, lettuce, mustard, onions, radishes, spinach, turnips, and watercress.

Chapter 5   Getting Warmer: the Importance of Compost*

One of the most important components of a sustainable fertile garden is a healthy supply of compost*. There are almost as many ways to make compost* as there are gardeners it seems. The number of choices and their pros and cons can feel overwhelming – just pick a method and go with it. Also bear in mind that many composting methods are severely slowed by a Zone 3 winter.

Basically there are three common composting methods: hot compost*, compost* tea, and cold compost*. Hot compost* is created in a pile that exceeds 125F and which also kills most of the weed seeds. It is usually considered an ideal, but requires a lot of tending and turning. (Many of the portable compost* barrel systems on the market claim to make hot compost*.) It also requires the appropriate amounts of water and an additional nitrogen source (like manure or bone meal). In the summer, this compost* can be ready in only a month or so. Usually hot compost* is kept in a pile or bin to keep everything together, and sometimes there are alternating layers of brown (soil) and green (decaying plants).

Compost* tea is made by filling a bucket half full of finished compost*, adding water, and then pouring off and using the water on plants. The water-soluble nutrients from the compost* are thus transferred to the water in the bucket. This is useful for young or sickly plants, especially when the weather is dry. The compost* may be soaked several times before most of the water-soluble nutrients are gone. Then, it should be added to the soil in the garden.

Cold compost* is created in a pile which doesn't get hot. It takes a long time, but it requires very little work. This is the kind of compost* I usually make. I start a pile one year and use it the next. If I end up with too much compost* from the previous year, I simply plant something in the old compost* pile that will cover it up – like squash or pumpkins. Wow, do they grow! And, because the compost* pile has been sitting on top of the ground for a year – no weeds!

Chapter 6   As the Dirt Turns: Crop Rotation* and Companion Plants

An important aspect of gardening sustainably is crop rotation*. Crop rotation* keeps the soil from being depleted in certain nutrients, and also prevents the buildup of disease in the soil because different plants are grown in it every year. Each area of your garden contains a micro-history of what was grown in it before, so continually changing what is grown stops the soil from being drained of the favorite micronutrients from a given crop. For example, carrots like boron*. If you keep growing carrots in the same place year after year eventually your carrots will grow poorly and become deformed due to boron* deficiency.

Crop rotation* is important, but it does not need to be particularly elaborate. I use a seven year rotation (peas, greens, beans, corn, squash, potatoes/roots, brassicas*) because the various categories all need similar amounts of garden space. Your rotation may be simpler, but it is important to keep the following in mind: plant a heavy feeder* like corn right after a legume (like peas or beans), and keep squash ahead of potatoes. Sometimes the odds and ends- type of plants just need to fit in wherever it is convenient.

Another consideration with crop rotation* is allowing a bed to be fallow* for a season or covering it with a cover crop* or green manure*. The cover crop* is then turned into the soil prior to planting the next new crop. Although it is not a planned part of my garden rotation, it is important to have cover crop* seeds at the ready in case of a crop failure. Cover crops* are much easier to turn under than weeds!

It is important to draw a map of your garden and number or name the various beds so a garden rotation is possible. You also need to document what you put into each bed, what the weather was like, how it grew, etc. Actually writing things down is boring, but it is the only way to accurately remember what happened. You will be surprised how important this information is when planning your garden next year.

My garden crop rotation* plan looks something like this:

Corn →	Beans →	Greens →	Peas ↓
Squash ↑	Greenhouse	Greenhouse	Brassicas* ↓
Path ↑	Pond	Pond	Potatoes/Roots ↓
↑	←←←←←←←←←	←←←←←←←←←	←←←←←←←←←

Yet another important aspect to crop rotation* is companion planting. Some plants grow well next to others, while other times there are plants which seem to fight and neither grows very well. A couple of classic examples of plant friends are: winter squash, corn, and beans (the Three Sisters in Native American lore). These are actually intermingled when planted, which may or may not work in your garden plan. Another famous pair of companion plants is: radishes and lettuce.

A couple of examples of plant foes: tomatoes and kohlrabi. For some reason they inhibit one another's growth if planted next to each other.

Vegetable	Preferred Soil Type	Plant Friends	Plant Foes
Green Bean	Sandy	Celery, Cucumber	None
Wax Bean	Sandy	Celery, Cucumber	None
Lima Bean	Sandy	Celery, Cucumber	None
Beet	Clay	Kohlrabi	None
Broccoli	Clay		None
Brussels Sprouts	Clay		None
Cabbage	Clay	Tomatoes	None
Cardoon	Sandy		None
Carrot	Clay for short, sandy for long	Peas	None
Cauliflower	Clay		None
Celeriac	Clay		None
Celery	Clay	Green Beans	None
Swiss Chard	Clay		None

Vegetable	Preferred Soil Type	Plant Friends	Plant Foes
Chinese Cabbage	Clay		None
Collards	Sandy		None
Corn	Sandy	Cucumbers	None
Cucumber	Sandy	Beans, Corn	None
Eggplant	Sandy	Basil	None
Garlic	Sandy		None
Kale	Clay		None
Kohlrabi	Clay	Beets	Tomatoes, Beans
Leek	Clay	Celery	None
Lettuce	Clay	Radishes	None
Muskmelon	Sandy		None
Mustard	Clay		None
Okra	Sandy		None
Onion	Clay	Beans	None
Parsnip	Clay		None
Pea	Clay	Carrots, Turnips	None
Hot Pepper	Sandy		None
Sweet Pepper	Sandy		None
Potato	Clay	Corn, Beans	None
Pumpkin	Sandy		None
Radish	Clay	Lettuce	None
Rutabaga	Clay		None
Spinach	Clay		None
Summer Squash	Sandy		None
Winter Squash	Sandy		None
Tomatillo	Sandy		None
Tomato	Sandy	Parsley, Cabbage	Kohlrabi, Fennel
Turnip	Clay	Peas	None
Watercress	Clay		None
Watermelon	Sandy		None
Zucchini	Sandy		None

Chapter 7   Caring for the Garden: Weeds, Water, and Weather

One of the most interesting and unpredictable aspects of gardening in Zone 3 is the weather. Weeds and water, on the other hand, are quite predictable. You will have to deal with both of them.

The best way to deal with weeds is to prevent them in the first place. This can be done by using mulch*, either natural (grass clippings, hay, compost*) or man-made (landscape fabric). When you plant seeds, though, the weeds already have a head start. A good way to slow them down initially is to cultivate the soil (multiple times if possible) where you plan to plant the seeds. Then apply mulch* in the area in between the rows. Once the seedlings are up and you are thinning* them anyway, you will need to weed in between them before adding mulch* to stop additional weeds. This works very well for plants like peas or beets.

Another way to get ahead of the weeds is to start your seeds in pots inside, and then later transplant the seedlings into the garden. Again, you want to cultivate the soil where you are planting prior to putting in the seedlings. This time, though, you can mulch* in between the rows and in between the plants all at once. It is important to keep the natural mulch* a little way away from the seedlings so they don't start to rot when you water them. This technique works well for tomatoes, peppers, and eggplants.

Inevitably, though, there will be times when weeding is necessary. That is when it is important to have a hoe that fits you. A narrow garden tiller works well for weeding also, but it will damage plant roots if it gets too close to them. I have used a 12" tiller with good success in my garden as long as the weeds are not too large. At some point, weeding by hand is necessary. Weeding by hand can be a wonderful contemplative experience, but it is definitely the slowest way to clean out the unwanted plants. It is the most effective, however.

Water is a critical component for healthy plants – not too much, not too little. This can be challenging – especially on clay-based soil. One of the biggest sources of frustration on clay based soil is the fact that it is very slow to warm up in the spring. You can put black plastic over the section of ground you want to heat up, but you should expect to have somewhat limited success because of the cool soil all around it.

Another helpful technique for dealing with water in a clay based soil is to build raised beds. Raised beds are sections of the garden that are higher than the surrounding paths. Sometimes they have sturdy walls to keep the soil up, sometimes they are only mounds. Both methods work, and both allow the soil to warm up faster in the spring. They also dry out faster, and in the fall they will freeze sooner than if the garden were flat. The walls for a raised bed need to be made from nontoxic materials so they don't leach anything into the soil. Examples of good materials to use for raised beds include: properly treated wood planks or bricks.

Some people use drip irrigation, which is run under the mulch* in a row where seedlings have been planted. It needs to be done before the plants are in the ground, and it is very effective at efficiently watering the row of plants. It is a little expensive, however, so that must be taken into consideration. Drip irrigation is helpful for sandy soil because everything needs to be watered so frequently.

One challenging aspect of the weather is the wind. Especially if the plants are just in the process of being hardened off*, the wind can cause significant damage to the leaves and stems. You need to remember to acclimate* your transplants to the wind conditions as well as the temperature conditions.

It is important to pay attention to the low temperatures, especially in the spring and early summer. Tender plants like tomatoes or peppers will actually stop growing for a while if the nights are too cold (anything below 60F). This problem can be mitigated by using a layer of glass, plastic or old bed sheets over the plants at night, and removing it during the day once it has warmed above 60F again.

Chapter 8   Baby, Baby: Starting Seeds Indoors

Because of the short growing season in Zone 3, it is usually a good idea to start as many plants inside as possible, then transplant them into the garden later. Commonly transplanted vegetables include: tomatoes, peppers, eggplant, broccoli, Brussels sprouts, cabbage, and cauliflower. Lettuces and other greens generally transplant well also. Other plants to consider transplanting are: beets, summer squash, and watermelon. Cucumbers and winter squash can be started inside and transplanted, but they are extremely fragile and transplanting them too roughly may cause them to die. The table in Chapter 4 indicates which plants do or do not transplant well.

It is important for the plants to be about the right size and the soil to be the right temperature when they are transitioned outside and planted. If they are too large and leggy* the stress of the move will set them back quite a bit. Planting them outside when the ground is either too cold or too warm doesn't work well either. A soil thermometer is a handy tool if it is available. Most plants have an ideal temperature range for growing well. See the table in this chapter for a more detailed listing of ideal plant growing temperatures for the various vegetables.

Using the data in chapter 4 and a calendar, you can roughly determine when to plant your vegetable seeds so they are about the right size when you want to take them outside. It is a good idea to write down when to start various plants so they are ready at the time you want them to be. Usually it is too busy in May and June to calculate when you want to start the crops for fall harvest, so consider doing it right away in March and early April when things are less busy in the garden. Put all of this information on the correct date on a calendar (with lots of room to add information) so it is easy to find.

Starting seeds is simple if you have a south facing window or fluorescent lighting that you have set up for plants. The ideal germination soil temperature for most plants is 75F, so a heat mat* can help get your seedlings off to a quicker start. Big seeds like cucumber, squash, and watermelon should be started in larger pots so as to disturb the roots as little as possible. Smaller seeds can be started in small pots and then transplanted later as they grow. Generally the smaller seeds will need to be growing longer anyway, and starting them out in small pots saves a lot of space initially. (Putting a seed or small plant into too large of a pot sometimes slows then down too.) Covering the seed trays with a clear plastic cover helps to retain the moisture, although you need to be alert for mold issues if the soil is too wet. Once the plants are tall enough, the clear plastic cover has to be removed so they can continue to grow.

Determining the correct potting soil to use can be a matter of significant debate. It is important to use soil which has not been treated with any artificial pesticides or herbicides; organic* potting soil would be the ideal. Organic* or all natural potting soil is available at many local hardware stores or garden centers. It is important to remember that growing seeds in the soil removes some of the nutrients, so used potting soil should be sent to the compost* pile once the plants have been transplanted.

Another type of soil frequently sold at plant centers is Germinating Soil. Germinating soil contains no fertilizer and is usually sterile. Germinating soil helps prevent disease in very young plants, especially damping off*, a disease where the young plants die right at the ground.

Regardless of the soil used, it is important to start with pots which have been sterilized or sanitized in order to limit diseases. This can be accomplished by washing the pots in a weak bleach solution (1/2 cup of bleach in 1 gallon water), or by submerging the pots in boiling water for at least 5 minutes.

Once the plants are large enough and the soil is warm enough (see the table below), it is time to harden* the plants off to get them ready for their life outside. It generally takes about a week to acclimate* the little babes to the great outdoors and to minimize the shock* of movement. On the first day, leave the plants outside in the shade and out of the wind for about an hour sometime in the mid afternoon if possible. On the second day, make it two hours, on the third day four hours, on day four six hours. On day five leave the plants out all day, but bring them in at night. On day 6 leave them out all day and overnight into day 7. On day 7 you should be able to plant them in the ground. If the weather has been extreme in the meantime, though, you might need to wait a bit. Base your decision on how the plants look. They will doubtless be stressed, but they shouldn't look overly so.

Vegetable	Preferred Soil Type	Ideal Soil Temperature
Green Bean	Sandy	65-75F
Wax Bean	Sandy	65-75F
Lima Bean	Sandy	70-80F
Beet	Clay	60-70F
Broccoli	Clay	60-70F
Brussels Sprouts	Clay	60-70F
Cabbage	Clay	60-70F
Cardoon	Sandy	70-80F
Carrot	Clay for short, sandy for long	65-80F
Cauliflower	Clay	65-70F
Celery	Clay	60-70F
Swiss Chard	Clay	60-70F
Chinese Cabbage	Clay	55-70F
Collards	Sandy	60-70F
Corn	Sandy	65-85F
Cucumber	Sandy	65-80F
Eggplant	Sandy	70-80F
Garlic	Sandy	60-70F
Kale	Clay	55-65F
Kohlrabi	Clay	60-70F
Leek	Clay	60-70F
Lettuce	Clay	60-70F
Muskmelon	Sandy	70-80F
Mustard	Clay	60-70F
Okra	Sandy	65-85F
Onion	Clay	60-80F
Parsnip	Clay	65-80F
Pea	Clay	55-70F
Hot Pepper	Sandy	70-85F
Sweet Pepper	Sandy	70-80F

Vegetable	Preferred Soil Type	Ideal Soil Temperature
Potato	Clay	55-70F
Pumpkin	Sandy	65-80F
Radish	Clay	55-65F
Rutabaga	Clay	55-70F
Spinach	Clay	55-65F
Summer Squash	Sandy	70-85F
Winter Squash	Sandy	70-85F
Tomatillo	Sandy	70-85F
Tomato	Sandy	70-80F
Turnip	Clay	55-70F
Watercress	Clay	55-65F
Watermelon	Sandy	70-80F
Zucchini	Sandy	70-80F

When planting, make sure to dig a deep enough hole so the plant can be surrounded by the garden soil, not just its own soil. It is a good idea to bury a part of the stems of leggy* plants in order to make them sturdier and have more roots. Don't forget to apply mulch* around them to minimize weeding later. Once planted, be sure to water them sufficiently and give them a bit of extra water for the next week or two until they are established. If they continue to look stressed, you might want to give them a shot of compost* tea or another liquid organic* fertilizer.

Chapter 9   Putting it All Together

Now that you have gathered all kinds of data about your garden plan, it is time to put it together. You should have the following:
1) List of plants you plan to grow
2) Approximate area needed for each type of plant and rough estimate of number of seeds needed
3) Garden Layout Plan (including crop rotations for future years)
4) Calendar of planting dates for plants you intend to start inside and transplant

Using the blank calendar you started to fill in Chapter 8, add the approximate dates for planting seeds which must be directly sown in the garden. All of this is weather dependent, of course, but at least it gives a general framework for when you must be planting in the garden. If you need to prepare any of the beds prior to planting, be sure to add that work somewhere on the calendar so it is not forgotten.

Next, write down all of the seeds you currently have and their age either in a spreadsheet or in a notebook. This is your seed inventory. Please bear in mind that many seeds are only viable for a couple of years, so plan to buy fresh seeds for planting in the garden if your seeds are more than two years old.

Then, check out your supplies of potting soil, small and medium and large pots, tools, etc. Based on your current seed inventory and your supply list, put together a shopping list of all that you will need to grow your desired garden. Seeds and supplies are available locally, but you might want to check out the seed and supply companies listed in Appendix D.

Get your seeds and supplies ordered and bought. Once you get them, put them all together in a convenient location which protects them from the elements (and pests like mice). A dedicated pest-proof bin with a lid is a very convenient way to keep all your seeds together. Store in a cool and dry location.

Keep all of your garden planning information together, and be sure to write down when you planted each crop, when you transplanted them, etc. Your seed planting calendar is a convenient location to write down how your garden progresses. It will also be a handy planning tool for next year.

That's it! Your garden plan is ready to go, so prepare to dig in as soon as the soil can be worked. And, of course, enjoy the fruits of your labor all throughout the year!

The rest of this book has some additional information about moving beyond the basic outside garden and extending the season either outside or inside the house. There is also a chapter on interesting and useful tips, tricks, and techniques gleaned from other gardeners in Zone 3.

Chapter 10   It's Not Too Late Yet: Season Extension

Because of the shortness of the growing season in Zone 3, everyone wants to extend how long crops can be grown. One of the simplest methods of season extension is to start the seeds indoors as indicated previously. This allows plants to be up to eight weeks old when placed in the garden.

Another method of season extension is to cover the soil with black plastic to help it heat up faster in the spring. This can extend the season by a couple of weeks, but probably not much longer.

A historical method for spring season extension is to dig a 2' deep trench in the fall. In the spring, add 6-12" of FRESH horse manure and another 12" of soil. The rotting manure will heat the soil to allow for earlier planting.

A cold frame* can also be used to protect the plants either in the spring or in the fall. It can extend the season by two to three weeks in the spring and by up to four weeks in the fall. A simple cold frame can be built of 2x4's and one 2x6 cut to fit the size of an old window to be used. If an old window is not available, heavy clear plastic connected to a frame can also be used.

Figure 5 Frame of Cold Frame placed on the soil

Figure 6 Cold Frame with Window on Top

Note the gap between the window and the frame to allow for cooling. If the night is to be cold, the window and this space should be covered either with a blanket or a tarp to keep the cold air out.

The most elaborate and expensive method of season extension is a greenhouse. It can extend the season by four to six weeks at the beginning and up to twelve weeks at the end (depending upon the weather). And, if it is heated it can be used most of the winter. The cost for heating will be prohibitive, though, unless there is an unusually mild winter. So, even with a greenhouse you should plan for some downtime in the winter from your gardening labors. It is important to orient the greenhouse east/west to take maximum advantage of the sunlight. Here is a picture of my Hoophouse greenhouse in March 2013. Note the cold frame on the right hand side in the interior picture.

Figure 7 Hoophouse Exterior March 2013

Figure 8 Hoophouse Interior March 2013

Realistically speaking, it works best to try to extend the back end of the season (i.e. longer period for harvest) rather than the front end. Most likely you will already be starting plants indoors or purchasing young plants, so the simple season extension on the front end is already done.

You should expect to extend the season on hardier vegetables only. Once it is 25F outside your squash, tomatoes and peppers will be frozen no matter what you do. The broccoli, spinach, cauliflower, turnips, carrots, beets, leeks, and kale can be protected to extend the season for a while. Brussels sprouts can handle some pretty cold weather (20F) so they can just stay out in the garden until you need them.

Here are a couple of techniques for keeping your vegetables going longer: 1) Put up a simple cold frame around them which you leave open during the day and close at night (use an old window or framed plastic as indicated in Figures 5 and 6); 2) cover the plants with loose straw or hay completely and uncover them during the day when it is warm enough to harvest them. Technique one works best for plants which have something above ground for you to harvest – like broccoli or kale. Technique 2 works for all of the hardier vegetables, but you must be careful when removing the straw or hay not to damage something you wish to harvest. Bear in mind that eventually the ground will freeze and you will have to be done harvesting for the year.

Another relatively low cost way to extend the season is to cover your vegetables with a low tunnel*. There are a number of designs for them available online, and one can be built for under $300. Floating row covers* can also be used, but they will not protect for as long as a sturdier structure like a cold frame or a low tunnel. You can also try using two layers of protection to get another couple of weeks out of your kale or spinach.

Chapter 11   Growing in the Winter: Sprouts and Forcing

Just because the weather is cold outside, it doesn't mean you have to stop growing good things to eat. Fresh, homegrown vegetables in the winter are a real treat. Sprouts, in particular, grow very quickly and can be ready in as little as 8-10 days for things like pea sprouts and sunflower sprouts. Usually, we don't think of eating the whole pea plant or the whole young sunflower, but they are quite delicious as a salad on a cold January night. We'll talk about them in detail next, but there are many kinds of sprouts – so this is just the beginning. Make sure that you always use UNTREATED seed.   Check the seed catalogs or your local food coop or grocery store for seeds and seed sprouting supplies.

Sprouts that you grow for their leaves and stems (like peas and sunflowers) will require some light so their leaves will be green. You can use the same place that you have your young plants in the spring and summer (south facing window or fluorescent lighting- even cheap lights will work just fine); as long as they get some light they will amaze you at how quickly they grow.

In order to start sprouts, you will need a mason jar with a lid with holes in it (either a special sprouting lid or one you make yourself). Add an appropriate amount of seed (4-12 TBSP depending on size of seed). Fill the jar with water and allow the seed to soak overnight. In the morning, drain and rinse the seed, leaving it moist but not in standing water. Rinse and drain the seed twice a day until you notice the roots starting to grow. Then, put about 1-1/2" of soil in a tray (I use the trays I have for starting my plants) and GENTLY spread the sprouted seeds on top. GENTLY work the seed just a little way into the soil. Cover with a clear cover and put in your sunny location.

Check the seedlings once or twice a day. Water if needed, trying not to splash dirt on the emerging leaves. If mold develops, leave the cover off for a while so it dries out a bit. Mold spores are ubiquitous, so having a little mold on the plants is a somewhat likely occurrence. Just be sure to dry things out so it doesn't spread too much. You are growing a lot of seeds in a small area so expect that you will have a living green carpet when it is time to harvest.

Once the shoots have reached 3" (for sunflowers) or 8-10" (for peas) it is time to enjoy them. For the sunflowers, gently pet the shoots to remove any clinging hulls. (The peas won't need to have this done because their hulls don't stick to the leaves.) Cut the stems close to the soil with either a scissors or a sharp knife. Rinse them if they got soil on the leaves. They are now ready to eat.

If you put the tray of cut seedlings back in your sunny locale, you should be able to get a second harvest in another 3-5 days. After that, they are too weak to put up another shoot and the soil and roots should be added to your compost* pile.

Another method of growing fresh greens in the winter is called forcing. With this method, you plant a dormant root and "force" it to grow leaves by putting it in a warm location (at least 50-60F) in a pot and water it like you want it to grow. Roots that work well for forcing are: witloof chicory (Belgian endive) asparagus, dandelion, and rhubarb. If you have stored beets or parsnips and they are starting to sprout, their leaves are edible also.

Chapter 12 Tips, Tricks, and Techniques

This is a compendium of ideas that can help make your garden grow better.

PESTS

If you have mice or voles* or birds eating your seeds when you plant them (I once had ducks follow me down the row eating my seeds), transplant seedlings instead. For some reason they seem to not like them nearly as much as the seeds themselves.

One way to get rid of slugs* is to place a saucer of beer near the affected plants. The slugs* crawl in, but cannot get out. You should plan to clean out the dead slugs* daily until no more appear.

Another way to prevent slugs* is to surround your plants (or even the whole bed) with a ring of copper. The slugs* get a shock when they try to cross it, so they don't.

Floating row covers* can be used to keep birds, rabbits, and some insects away from cabbage worm prone plants like cauliflower, kale, broccoli or cabbage. Cabbage worms turn into beautiful white moths, but they leave the leaves of their plant victims full of holes. If you see the moths you need to take immediate action to save your veggies.

If you have a problem with rabbits in your garden, the best (and practically only) way to protect your plants is to build a rabbit-proof fence around them. The fence will need to be at least three feet tall and have holes too small for a rabbit to get through (2"x4"). Floating row covers* sometimes help. Surrounding the plants with blood meal sometimes helps also.

Deer are much harder to stop than rabbits in the garden. An eight foot tall fence is the most effective deterrent, but it is very expensive. A line of electric fence run about three feet off the ground sometimes keeps out deer. An additional line at six or seven feet off the ground may be needed if the deer continue to be determined to get into the garden.

Another deer deterrent if you have the space is to lay a 4' tall piece of chicken wire flat on the ground surrounding the area you want to protect. The chicken wire hurts the deer's hooves, so they tend to stay away.

Powdered cayenne pepper or liquid pepper spray can also deter rabbits and deer.

The best solution to limit potato bugs is to plant the potatoes later in the season. Otherwise the best way to deal with them is to pick them off the plants.

SEED STARTING AND TRANSPLANTING TIPS

Germinate inside, grow outside.

Consider soaking seeds overnight prior to planting to speed germination. This is particularly helpful for the larger seeds like beans or peas.

Many gardeners plant according to the moon's cycle. Plant root vegetables (beets, carrots, rutabaga) when moon is going down (waning), and the vegetables which you harvest above the ground (lettuce, kale, cabbage) when moon is growing (waxing).

Let many of the "volunteer" plants (plants that sprouted from last year's garden), especially herbs, grow unless you have big plans for their location.

If you get tomato transplants from the store, choose leggy* specimens and bury most of the stem. The buried stem will sprout roots and make for a stronger and more vigorous plant.

If you buy a tomato plant from the store that has already set fruit, bear in mind that the fruit already set will continue to ripen, but more fruit will not set any earlier than a much smaller plant.

You can use old plastic milk jugs with the bottoms cut out to protect young seedlings from pests or the wind.

Patience in germination is vital. Sometimes it takes seeds a lot longer to germinate than you might expect. Especially if the soil is a little too cool, seeds may take up to twice as long to germinate as indicated on the package.

WATERING AND WEED CONTROL

Black plastic is an excellent mulch* because it heats up the soil and deters weeds. But, rather than cover your entire garden with a big sheet of black plastic (which will be bothered by the wind), lay the black plastic in strips and cut holes in the strip to insert your already growing plants. In between the strips, keep weeds down with a lawn mower. Ground stakes are also available at garden centers for securing the plastic to the ground.

Sometimes putting down mulch* or black plastic too early will keep the soil too cool, and slow plant growth. Mulch* shouldn't be put down until the soil temperature is at least 50F.

Red plastic works better than black plastic for tomatoes for many growers. If you are a tomato fan, it is worth a try.

If you decide to use domestic birds for weed control, use ducks rather than chickens. Chickens scratch at the ground, digging up young plants in their search for bugs. Ducks will leave fertilizer for you, however, so be sure to wash all vegetables thoroughly before eating them.

Bantam chickens or guinea fowl can be used for tick control to good effect as long as the plants in the garden are of sufficient size to prevent damage from their scratching the ground.

An old glass bottle can be used to keep a plant watered on hot days. Fill the bottle with water and stick it (neck down) into the soil near the plant needing to be watered. The water will empty slowly enough to keep the plant refreshed all day.

Trim low branches of tomato plants away so that blight cannot climb up the plant from the ground. Stirring the soil every couple of weeks near where the tomato vine comes out of the ground also slows or stops blight.

SEED STORAGE

If you decide to save your own seeds, use washed pill bottles for storage. They are compact, seal tightly, and many of them block out Ultraviolet light.

SEASON EXTENSION

Big black barrels full of water can keep a nearby area up to 5-10F warmer. The water warms during the day and releases the heat slowly at night. The barrel may get mold in it, so it should NOT be used to water plants.

Planting somewhat tender plants in a sheltered area may allow some Zone 4 plants to survive in Zone 3.

A simple plan for the soil inside a 3' tall raised bed is: 1' sand on the bottom, 1' soil in the middle, and 1' composted manure on top.

Black plastic can be held to the sides of a wooden raised bed by nailing slats (1" wide thin pieces of wood three or four feet long) around the edge of the raised bed with the black plastic between the slats and the wood of the bed.

Appendix A USDA Hardiness Zone Map

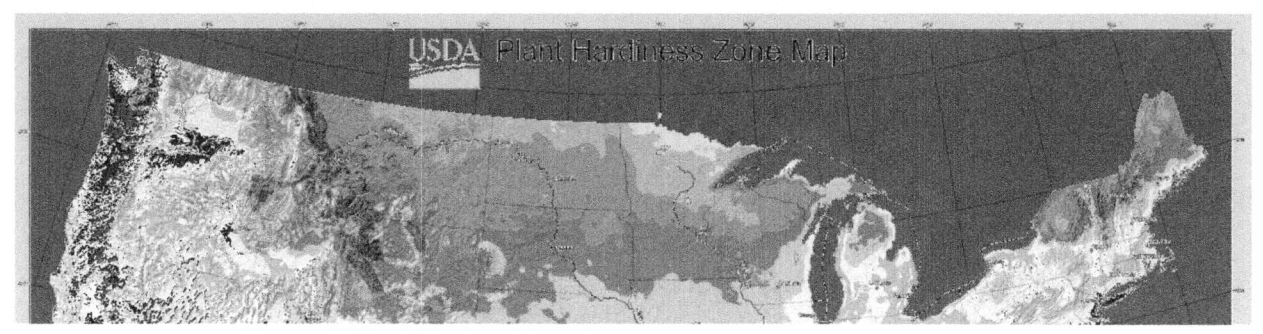

Figure 5 USDA Hardiness Zone Map 2012

Shaded areas indicate Zone 3 or 4.

Worldwide Hardiness Zone Map available at: http://tcpermaculture.blogspot.com

Appendix B Theme Gardens

Salsa Garden - Tomatoes, hot peppers, sweet peppers, garlic, onions, cilantro

Potato Salad Garden – Potatoes, onions, celery, carrots, parsley

Pickle Garden – Cucumbers, onions, garlic, hot peppers, dill

Southern Garden –Tomatoes, okra, collards, onions, watermelon

Russian Garden – Beets, potatoes, cabbage, kohlrabi, onions

Tex-Mex Garden – Tomatoes, hot peppers, sweet peppers, garlic, tomatillos

Sauerkraut Garden – cabbage, onions, carrots, caraway

Greek Garden – Tomatoes, cucumbers, hot peppers, eggplant, okra, spinach, basil

Italian Garden – Tomatoes, sweet peppers, cucumbers, eggplant, spinach, oregano

Oriental Garden – Chinese cabbage, onions, garlic, carrots, celery, cilantro

Appendix C Vegetable Quantity Calculation Guide

Vegetable	Variety	Amt/week	Weeks per season	No. Plants	Spacing	Row feet needed**
Green Bean	Bush	2 qt	8	20	6"	10
Wax Bean	Pole	2 qt	8	15	9"	10
Lima Bean	Bush	2 qt	4	20	9"	10
Beet	Detroit	1 qt	12	120	3"	40
Broccoli	Waltham	1 head	12	24	12"	24
Brussels Sprouts	Long Island	1 qt	8	24	12"	24
Cabbage	Dutch Late	1 head	6	12	12"	12
Cardoon	Porto Spless	1 qt	6	24	18"	36
Carrot	Danvers	10	12	120	4"	40
Cauliflower	Snowball	1 head	6	12	12"	12
Celeriac		1 root	8	16	12"	16
Celery	Utah	1 head	6	6	18"	9
Swiss Chard	Fordhook	1 qt	10	30	9"	21
Chinese Cabbage		1 head	8	8	9"	6
Collards	Vates	1 qt	8	24	12"	24
Corn	Silver Qn	1 doz	6	100	18"	150
Cucumber	Swt Success	3 cukes	4	4	24"	8
Eggplant	Blk Beauty	6	4	6	18"	9
Garlic		1 head	6	6	12"	6
Kale	Red Russian	1 qt	10	4	12"	4
Kohlrabi	Kossack	1 head	6	6	18"	9
Leek	Am Flag	3 heads	6	54	6"	27
Lettuce	Buttercrunch	3 heads	8	24	6"	12
Muskmelon	Athena	1	4	8	24"	16
Mustard	India Giant	1 qt	8	24	9"	18
Okra	Clemson	12	6	24	9"	18
Onion	Lisbon	10	12	120	4"	30
Parsnip	Harris	10	8	80	6"	40
Pea	Sugar Ann	1 qt	6	30	4"	20

Vegetable	Variety	Amt/ week	Weeks per season	No. Plants	Spacing	Row feet needed**
Hot Pepper	Thai Hot	10	6	2	12"	2
Sweet Pepper	King North	5	6	10	12"	10
Potato	Yukon Gold	2lb	10	10	24"	20
Pumpkin	Amish Pie	1 head	4	2	36"	6
Radish	Crimson Gl	10	15	150	4"	50
Rutabaga	Laurentian	2	12	24	6"	12
Spinach	Tyee	1 qt	12	48	6"	24
Summer Squash	Dixie	6	8	4	24"	8
Winter Squash	Kabocha	2	4	4	36"	12
Tomatillo	Tomaverde	12	4	6	12"	6
Tomato	Roma	2 qt	6	8	24"	16
Turnip	Purple Top	12	12	160	3"	40
Watercress	Nastur Offic.	1 qt	8	20	6"	10
Watermelon	Sugar Baby	2	4	4	24"	8
Zucchini	Black	6	8	2	24"	4

**The Row Feet* are based on a 30" row. Remember when calculating the row feet* needed that more than one crop can be grown in the same row in a single season.

DISCLAIMER: These are the average results of my garden and my clay soil. My garden yields vary significantly from year to year based on weather conditions. You should expect your yields to vary also.

Appendix D Sources for Seeds and Planting Supplies

AM Leonard Horticultural Tool and Supply 241 Fox Drive Piqua, Ohio 45356 USA
(800) 543-8955   http://amleo.com

W. Atlee Burpee & Co. 300 Park Avenue Warminster, PA 18974
(800) 888-1447   www.burpee.com

Gurney's Seed & Nursery Co P.O. Box 4178 Greendale, IN 47025-4178
(812) 260-2153   www.gurneys.com

Johnnys Selected Seeds 955 Benton Avenue Winslow, Maine 04901 USA
(877) 564-6697   http://Johnnyseeds.com

Jordan Seeds 6400 Upper Afton Rd Woodbury, Minnesota 55125 USA
(651) 738-3422   www.jordanseeds.com

J.W. Jung Seed Company 335 S. High St Randolph, WI 53956
(800) 297-3123   www.jungseed.com

Pinetree Garden Seeds and Accessories PO Box 300 Gloucester, Maine 04260 USA
(207) 926-3400   www.superseeds.com

Potato Garden 12101 2135 Rd Austin, Colorado 81410 USA
(877) 313-7783   www.potatogarden.com

RH Shumway Seeds 334 W Stroud St Randolph, WI 53956
(800) 342-9461   www.rhshumway.com

Seedway 99 Industrial Rd Elizabethtown, PA 17022 USA
(800) 952-7333   www.seedway.com

Stokes Seeds PO Box 548 Buffalo NY 14240-0548
(800) 396-9238   www.stokeseeds.com

Appendix E Bibliography and Further Reading

Ambler, Wayne <u>Treasury of Gardening</u> Publications International Copyright 1994 ISBN 0-7853-0650-1

Ashton, Jeff <u>The 12 –Month Gardener</u> Lark Books Copyright 2001 ISBN 1-57990-384-3

Bartholomew, Mel <u>All New Square Foot Gardening</u> Cool Springs Press Copyright 1985, 2001 ISBN 978-1-59186-202-4

Brauenstein, Mark <u>Sprout Garden</u> Book Publishing Co Copyright 1999 ISBN 978-1-57067-073-2

Bubel, Mike and Nancy <u>Root Cellaring</u> Storey Publishing Copyright 1991 ISBN 0-88266-703-3

Bubel, Nancy <u>Seed Starters Handbook</u> Rodale Press Copyright 1978 ISBN 0-87857-209-0

Coleman, Eliot <u>New Organic Grower</u> Chelsea Green Publishing copyright 1989 ISBN 0-930031-75-x

Coleman, Eliot <u>Winter Harvest Handbook</u> Chelsea Green Publishing copyright 2009 ISBN 978-1-60358-081-6

Flowerdew, Bob <u>Grow Your Own Eat Your Own</u> Kyle Books Copyright 2008 ISBN 978-1-906868-13-0

Harrington, Geri <u>Growing Chinese Vegetables</u> Storey Publishing Copyright 2009 ISBN 978-1-60342-140-9

Jabs, Carolyn <u>Heirloom Gardener</u> Sierra Club Books Copyright 1984 ISBN 0-87156-803-9

Martin, Deborah and Gershuny, Grace Editors <u>Rodale Book of Composting</u> Rodale Press Copyright 1992 ISBN 0-87857-991-5

Reich, Lee <u>Weedless Gardening</u> Workman Publishing Copyright 2001 ISBN 978-0-7611-1696-7

Rodale, J I Editor Encyclopedia of Organic Gardening Rodale Press Copyright 1970 Standard Book number 87596-061-8

Seymour, John The Self Sufficient Gardener Doubleday Copyright 1978 ISBN 0-381-14671-x

Stout, Ruth No-Work Garden Book Rodale Press Copyright 1971 Standard Book Number 0-87857-000-4

Yepsen, Roger JR Editor Encyclopedia of Natural Insect & Disease Control Rodale Press Copyright 1984 ISBN 0-87857-488-3

Yepsen, Roger JR Editor Organic Plant Protection Rodale Press Copyright 1976 ISBN 0-87857-110-8

Appendix F Glossary

Acclimate – method for minimizing shock to plants when transplanting by gradually getting them used to new conditions

Aerate – to add air (into the soil)

Bantam Chicken – small breed of chicken useful for eating wood ticks in gardens

Blanch – process of tying up leaves around the stalk of a plant to keep the sunlight away from the stalk in order to keep it more tender (celery or chicory) or burying a stalk to keep it white (leeks)

Bolt – the process of a plant going directly to seed and not producing a harvestable crop like roots (beets) or leaves (spinach)

Boron – element needed by many plants and sometimes lacking in the soil

Brassicas – member of the cabbage family – this includes cabbage, cauliflower, broccoli, Brussels sprouts, kale, turnips, rutabaga, kohlrabi, mustard, collards

Compost – rotted plant matter

Cover Crop – plants grown specifically to cover a garden bed for a season – usually tilled under for additional organic matter in the soil

Crop Rotation – process of moving crops from one bed to another over the course of years or seasons

Damping Off – a plant disease where the plant rots off right where it enters the ground- can be a problem when starting seeds indoors in pots or trays

Decomposed – compost broken down by bacteria to the point that its nutrients are available to plants

Fallow – not in cultivation

Floating Row Cover – portable lightweight cover that lets in light but protects plants from insects or frost

Green Manure – plant grown specifically to be tilled into the soil later to improve it

Harden Off – process of bringing a plant into and out of the house in order to ease the transition to being planted outside

Heat Mat – electric device used underneath pots to heat the soil to speed germination and growth

Heavy Feeder – plant which requires a significant amount of fertilizer (or compost) in order to grow well

Indeterminate – plant which has a vine-like stem which must be supported (Many kinds of peas, beans, and tomatoes are indeterminate.)

Leggy – plant with an excessively long stem due to growing too far from a light source

Low Tunnel - two to four foot high clear or white cover used to protect crops in cold weather. It is usually portable and used only part of the season. The cover is held up by hoops stuck in the ground so cover does not touch the crop

Microclimate – small area that has a different climate than the area surrounding it (e.g. area next to a large body of water doesn't get as hot or as cold as the area further away from the water)

Mole – rodent that digs up plants looking for bugs in the soil. They cause damage by disturbing the roots and by putting air next to the roots – looks similar to vole

Mulch – ground covering use to either heat or cool the soil, and often used to prevent weed growth – it can be either man-made (e.g. landscape fabric) or naturally occurring (e.g. hay, straw, grass clippings)

Organic (matter)– naturally occurring plant or animal matter that rots to make compost

pH – measurement used to determine acidity of the soil – 7 is neutral, above 7 is basic, and below 7 is acidic

Row Feet – method of determining how much garden space needs to be used for a given crop to get a desired yield at harvest

Set Heads – process in broccoli, cauliflower, Brussels sprouts of developing their edible portions

Shock – process of upsetting a plant by changing its environment too quickly

Slug – shell-less snail that eats leaves of plants

Succession Planting – planting more than one crop of something in order to have a longer period of harvest, or planting a different crop in the same area during the course of a season

Thinning – process of removing extra seedlings so that remaining plants can grow better (For example, beet seeds contain several seeds in each cluster. Once they start growing some must be removed in order for the rest to grow to an acceptable size)

Tuber – Rhizome (root growth) used to start certain plants such as potatoes

Vole – rodent which eats seeds and young plants – looks similar to mole

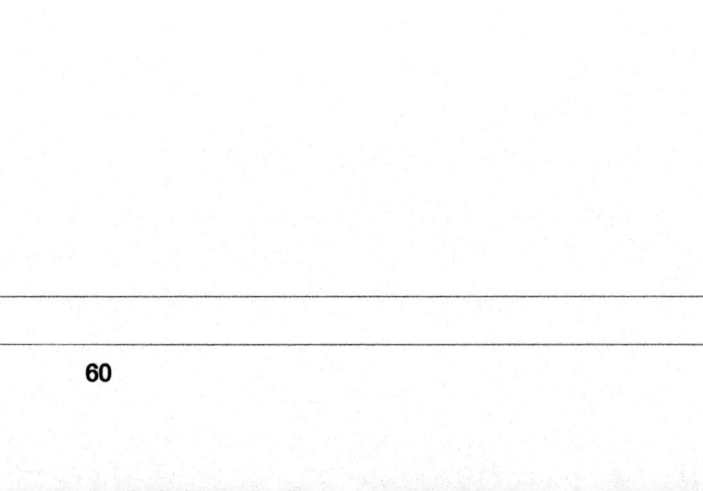

Made in the USA
Monee, IL
30 November 2020